Warm-ups

Ask your teacher to make a list of warm-ups for you to choose from when you begin each practice session (or see fabermusic.com/improve for some suggestions). These will include ideas on posture and hand position, playing without tension and a range of technical exercises.

Choose two or three warm-ups at the beginning of *every* practice session and spend at least two to three minutes on them.

Explore your piece

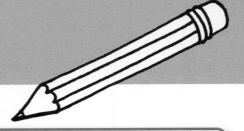

1 Title PRELUDE IN D♭ Major, Opus 28, No. 15 (RAINDROP)

2 Composer FRÉDÉRIC CHOPIN

3 Period Romantic (1810—1849)

See page 24 for help

4 What does the title tell you about the music?

WEATHER ELEMENTS. INTRODUCTION.

5 What key is the piece in? Are there any modulations in the piece? Which keys does it travel through?

D♭ Major. Yes—C♯ MINOR (ENHARMONIC)

6 Are there any scale and arpeggio patterns (including dominant and diminished 7ths) in the music? In which bars do they occur?

ARPEGGIP PATTERNS   BAR 1 (D♭ Maj), BAR 5 (D♭ Maj) Bar 9 (A♭ Maj)
BAR 10 (G♭ Maj) + (D♭ Maj), BARS 12/13 (A♭ Minor), BAR 14 (E♭ min) + (B♭ min)
DOMINANT A♭ (Bar 1, 5,

7 Are there any sequences in the piece?

R

8 Explain the time signature. Does it change? What will you count?

$\frac{4}{4}$ = 4 crochets in each measure. No.

9 Write down all the markings (e.g. articulation, accentuation, ornamentation etc.) and their meanings:

LIGHT AND SPIKEY BAR(S) 1—8. HEAVY IN BARS 36, 37, 38, 39, 40,
41, 42, 43, 44

Improve your practice!

Piano Grade **5**

Paul Harris

www.fabermusic.com/improve

© 2004 by Faber Music Ltd
First published in 2004 by Faber Music Ltd
3 Queen Square London WC1N 3AU
Design by Susan Clarke
Printed in England by Caligraving Ltd

ISBN 0-571-52265-3

FABER *ff* MUSIC

Introduction

You've probably heard the expression 'practice makes perfect'. But it's not just the quantity of practice that's important; it's the quality. With the aid of *Improve your practice!*, you will begin to develop ways of making the most out of your practice sessions – however long they are. What's more, you'll also find that your wider musical skills of aural, theory, sight-reading, improvisation and composition develop alongside.

Before you start

Using scissors, cut each playing card to size. As you work through each grade, add the new cards to your deck so you have even more to choose from.

1 Be a musical detective

When you begin a new piece, first complete *Explore your piece*. You may want to fill in all the boxes in one go or spread your detective work over a week or two.

2 Warm up

Begin each practice session with some warm-ups. Your teacher will write some down on the warm-ups page for you to choose from.

3 Without music

Choose the piece you are going to focus on in your practice and deal yourself two to three cards from the 'Without music' pack. Work through the activities without looking at the music.

4 With music

Now (using the same piece) deal yourself between two to four cards from the 'With music' pack and work through those activities with the music open.

5 You choose

Complete your practice with a further activity of your own choice – playing one of your other pieces, some other scales, doing some sight-reading, composing a piece – and always be thinking about what the week's special feature might be (see page 20).

important

You may want to concentrate on just one piece in a practice session, or perhaps work at several. Deal yourself different cards for each piece.

All these answers form the 'ingredients' of your piece. If you don't understand a question, don't worry: just remember to ask your teacher in your next lesson.

10 Write down all the dynamics. Ask your teacher if there are sufficient markings to give a stylistic performance. You may consider adding more of your own.

SOSTENUTO, SOTTO VOCE, SMORZANDO, SLENTANDO, RITENUTO, SF, FF, P, pedal, Accents.

11 How would you describe the character or mood of the piece? Does it remain the same throughout? How will you communicate this in your performance?

FIRST SECTION UP TO BAR 27 IS SLEEPY, GENTLE AND LIGHT. THE MIDDLE SECTION IS BUILDING UP TO A BODY GOING CLIMAX; VERY VIOLENT IN SOME PARTS (THUNDERSTORM) OR THROUGH DEATH PROCESS. LAST SECTION, THUNDER & LIGHTNING IS OVER, THE PEACE AND QUITENESS HAS BEEN RESTORED, AND THE RAIN VERY GRADUALLY TAILS OFF, UNTIL IT STOPS.

12 Find out something interesting about the composer:

SHORT LIFE-SPAN BUT ACCOMPLISHED A LOT.

13 Can you find another composer who writes in the same style?

SCHUMANN AND MENDELSSOHN

14 Are there any particular rhythms or repeated rhythmic patterns in the piece? Write them down here, and then clap them:

YES: BAR(S) 1, 3, 4, 5, 7, 8, 10, 14,

15 What are the technical challenges in the piece?

KEEPING THE RAINDROP (AKA A♭) IN LEFT HAND SOFT, LIGHT AND CLEAR SO MELODY CAN BE HEARD IN BARS 1-27. BRINGING OUT THE MELODY IN THE LEFT HAND FROM BARS 28 ONWARDS AND KEEPING THE RAINDROP IN RIGHT HAND SOFT BUT CLEAR.

16 Which bars will require special practice?

BAR(S) 4, 14, 15, 23, 37, 38, 62, 64, 65, 66, 70, 71, 72, 73, 74, 75, 79

Explore your piece

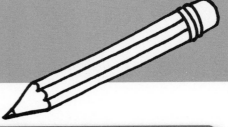

1 **Title** THE ENTERTAINER (DEDICATED TO JAMES BROWN AND HIS MANDOLIN CLUB

2 **Composer** SCOTT JOPLIN

3 **Period**

See page 24 for help

4 **What does the title tell you about the music?**

C.MAJOR.

5 **What key is the piece in? Are there any modulations in the piece? Which keys does it travel through?**

C.MAJOR. YES – F MAJOR

6 **Are there any scale and arpeggio patterns (including dominant and diminished 7ths) in the music? In which bars do they occur?**

ARPEGGIO PATTERN (BAR 61)

7 **Are there any sequences in the piece?**

8 **Explain the time signature. Does it change? What will you count?**

$\frac{2}{4}$ = 2 Crochets to each Bar. No. 1e+a 2e+a

9 **Write down all the markings (e.g. articulation, accentuation, ornamentation etc.) and their meanings:**

10 Write down all the dynamics. Ask your teacher if there are sufficient markings to give a stylistic performance. You may consider adding more of your own.

11 How would you describe the character or mood of the piece? Does it remain the same throughout? How will you communicate this in your performance?

12 Find out something interesting about the composer:

13 Can you find another composer who writes in the same style?

14 Are there any particular rhythms or repeated rhythmic patterns in the piece? Write them down here, and then clap them:

15 What are the technical challenges in the piece?

16 Which bars will require special practice?

Bar(s) 10, 11, 12,

Explore your piece

1 **Title** — I've Got You Under My Skin

2 **Composer** — Cole Porter

3 **Period** — 20ᵗʰ Century

See page 24 for help

4 **What does the title tell you about the music?**

Romantic

5 **What key is the piece in? Are there any modulations in the piece? Which keys does it travel through?**

E♭ Major — Yes   C Minor / F Major

6 **Are there any scale and arpeggio patterns (including dominant and diminished 7ths) in the music? In which bars do they occur?**

7 **Are there any sequences in the piece?**

8 **Explain the time signature. Does it change? What will you count?**

9 **Write down all the markings (e.g. articulation, accentuation, ornamentation etc.) and their meanings:**

10 Write down all the dynamics. Ask your teacher if there are sufficient markings to give a stylistic performance. You may consider adding more of your own.

11 How would you describe the character or mood of the piece? Does it remain the same throughout? How will you communicate this in your performance?

12 Find out something interesting about the composer:

13 Can you find another composer who writes in the same style?

14 Are there any particular rhythms or repeated rhythmic patterns in the piece? Write them down here, and then clap them:

15 What are the technical challenges in the piece?

16 Which bars will require special practice?

Explore your piece

1 Title

2 Composer

3 Period

See page 24 for help

4 What does the title tell you about the music?

5 What key is the piece in? Are there any modulations in the piece? Which keys does it travel through?

6 Are there any scale and arpeggio patterns (including dominant and diminished 7ths) in the music? In which bars do they occur?

7 Are there any sequences in the piece?

8 Explain the time signature. Does it change? What will you count?

9 Write down all the markings (e.g. articulation, accentuation, ornamentation etc.) and their meanings:

10 Write down all the dynamics. Ask your teacher if there are sufficient markings to give a stylistic performance. You may consider adding more of your own.

11 How would you describe the character or mood of the piece? Does it remain the same throughout? How will you communicate this in your performance?

12 Find out something interesting about the composer:

13 Can you find another composer who writes in the same style?

14 Are there any particular rhythms or repeated rhythmic patterns in the piece? Write them down here, and then clap them:

15 What are the technical challenges in the piece?

16 Which bars will require special practice?

Explore your piece

1. **Title**

2. **Composer**

3. **Period**

See page 24 for help

4. **What does the title tell you about the music?**

5. **What key is the piece in? Are there any modulations in the piece? Which keys does it travel through?**

6. **Are there any scale and arpeggio patterns (including dominant and diminished 7ths) in the music? In which bars do they occur?**

7. **Are there any sequences in the piece?**

8. **Explain the time signature. Does it change? What will you count?**

9. **Write down all the markings (e.g. articulation, accentuation, ornamentation etc.) and their meanings:**

10 Write down all the dynamics. Ask your teacher if there are sufficient markings to give a stylistic performance. You may consider adding more of your own.

11 How would you describe the character or mood of the piece? Does it remain the same throughout? How will you communicate this in your performance?

12 Find out something interesting about the composer:

13 Can you find another composer who writes in the same style?

14 Are there any particular rhythms or repeated rhythmic patterns in the piece? Write them down here, and then clap them:

15 What are the technical challenges in the piece?

16 Which bars will require special practice?

Explore your piece

1 Title

2 Composer

3 Period

See page 24 for help

4 What does the title tell you about the music?

5 What key is the piece in? Are there any modulations in the piece? Which keys does it travel through?

6 Are there any scale and arpeggio patterns (including dominant and diminished 7ths) in the music? In which bars do they occur?

7 Are there any sequences in the piece?

8 Explain the time signature. Does it change? What will you count?

9 Write down all the markings (e.g. articulation, accentuation, ornamentation etc.) and their meanings:

10 Write down all the dynamics. Ask your teacher if there are sufficient markings to give a stylistic performance. You may consider adding more of your own.

11 How would you describe the character or mood of the piece? Does it remain the same throughout? How will you communicate this in your performance?

12 Find out something interesting about the composer:

13 Can you find another composer who writes in the same style?

14 Are there any particular rhythms or repeated rhythmic patterns in the piece? Write them down here, and then clap them:

15 What are the technical challenges in the piece?

16 Which bars will require special practice?

Explore your piece

1 Title

2 Composer

3 Period

See page 24 for help

4 What does the title tell you about the music?

5 What key is the piece in? Are there any modulations in the piece? Which keys does it travel through?

6 Are there any scale and arpeggio patterns (including dominant and diminished 7ths) in the music? In which bars do they occur?

7 Are there any sequences in the piece?

8 Explain the time signature. Does it change? What will you count?

9 Write down all the markings (e.g. articulation, accentuation, ornamentation etc.) and their meanings:

10 Write down all the dynamics. Ask your teacher if there are sufficient markings to give a stylistic performance. You may consider adding more of your own.

11 How would you describe the character or mood of the piece? Does it remain the same throughout? How will you communicate this in your performance?

12 Find out something interesting about the composer:

13 Can you find another composer who writes in the same style?

14 Are there any particular rhythms or repeated rhythmic patterns in the piece? Write them down here, and then clap them:

15 What are the technical challenges in the piece?

16 Which bars will require special practice?

Explore your piece

1 **Title**

2 **Composer**

3 **Period**

See page 24 for help

4 **What does the title tell you about the music?**

5 **What key is the piece in? Are there any modulations in the piece? Which keys does it travel through?**

6 **Are there any scale and arpeggio patterns (including dominant and diminished 7ths) in the music? In which bars do they occur?**

7 **Are there any sequences in the piece?**

8 **Explain the time signature. Does it change? What will you count?**

9 **Write down all the markings (e.g. articulation, accentuation, ornamentation etc.) and their meanings:**

10 Write down all the dynamics. Ask your teacher if there are sufficient markings to give a stylistic performance. You may consider adding more of your own.

11 How would you describe the character or mood of the piece? Does it remain the same throughout? How will you communicate this in your performance?

12 Find out something interesting about the composer:

13 Can you find another composer who writes in the same style?

14 Are there any particular rhythms or repeated rhythmic patterns in the piece? Write them down here, and then clap them:

15 What are the technical challenges in the piece?

16 Which bars will require special practice?

Practice diary

As your practice develops each week, decide on one special feature.

It may, for example, be one of the following:

· part or all of one of your pieces that you can play really well
· a technical challenge that you've overcome
· an improvisation (one that you can remember!)
· a particular scale you can play really well
· your own composition

Write it down in the table below and show it to your teacher.

It will become a very good starting point for the next lesson.

Week beginning	This week's special feature

Exam checklist

You may want to work through this section with your teacher.

Scales and arpeggios
List all the scales etc. you need to know for the exam, or those that you are currently working on:

Aural
List the different tests you'll need to do:

Countdown to an exam

Tick each statement as soon as you feel it to be true! Award yourself a treat when all are ticked.

3 weeks to go ...

○ I can play all my scales slowly but accurately, rhythmically and with a good and even tone.

○ I'm practising sight-reading every day.

○ I know exactly what the aural tests require me to do and have had a lot of help with them.

○ I can play my pieces fairly fluently and with expression.

2 weeks to go ...

○ I can play all my scales slowly but accurately and fluently.

○ I'm practising sight-reading every day.

○ I've had a lot of practice at the aural tests.

○ I can play my pieces fluently, with expression and character.

1 week to go ...

○ I can play all my scales accurately, fluently and confidently.

○ I'm still practising sight-reading every day.

○ I'm confident about the aural tests.

○ I've performed all my pieces to friends/relatives confidently and with lots of musical expression and character.

1 day to go ...

○ I'm really looking forward to the exam and am going to get a good night's sleep!

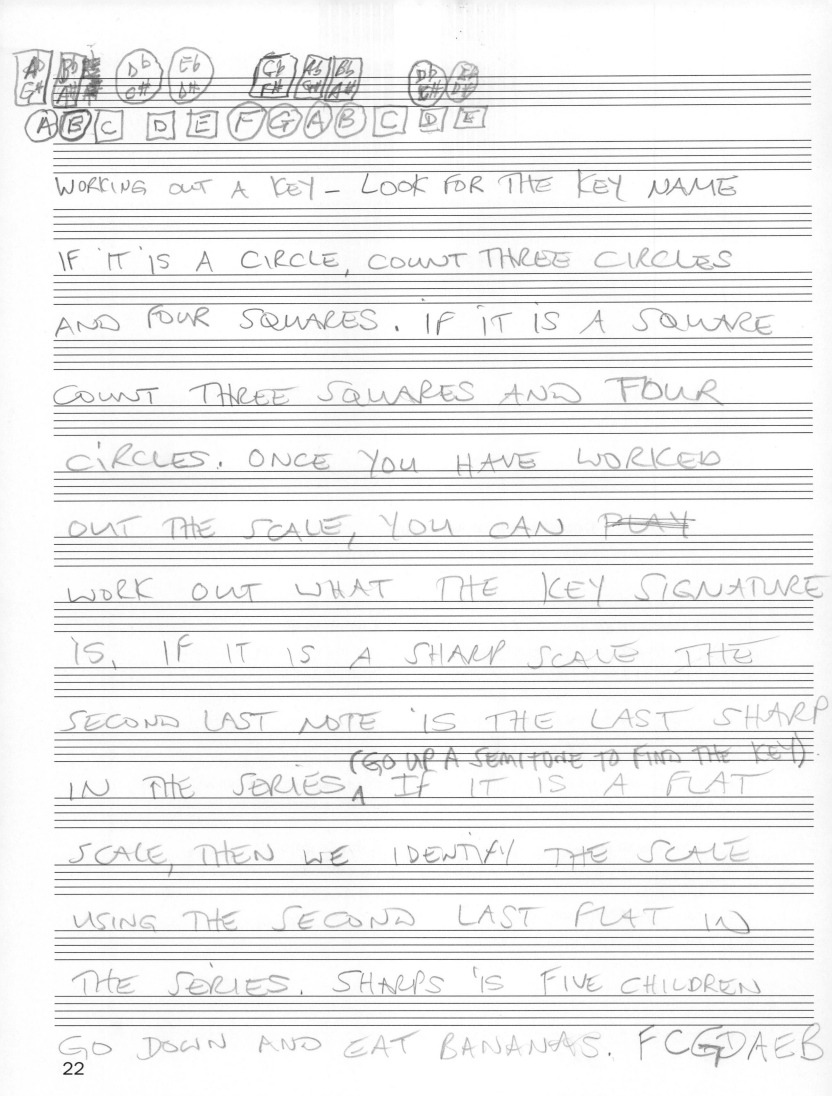

WORKING OUT A KEY — LOOK FOR THE KEY NAME

IF IT IS A CIRCLE, COUNT THREE CIRCLES

AND FOUR SQUARES. IF IT IS A SQUARE

COUNT THREE SQUARES AND FOUR

CIRCLES. ONCE YOU HAVE WORKED

OUT THE SCALE, YOU CAN ~~PLAY~~

WORK OUT WHAT THE KEY SIGNATURE

IS, IF IT IS A SHARP SCALE THE

SECOND LAST NOTE IS THE LAST SHARP

IN THE SERIES. (GO UP A SEMITONE TO FIND THE KEY) IF IT IS A FLAT

SCALE, THEN WE IDENTIFY THE SCALE

USING THE SECOND LAST FLAT IN

THE SERIES. SHARPS IS FIVE CHILDREN

GO DOWN AND EAT BANANAS. F C G D A E B

THE FLATS SERIES IS: BANANAS
EATEN AFTER DINNER GIVE CHILDREN
FAT. BEADGCF. IT IS A
REVERSE OF THE SHARPS.

Useful stuff

Bear in mind that these dates are intended as a guide only.

Composer dates	Period
c.1425–1600	Renaissance
c.1600–1750	Baroque
c.1750–1820	Classical
c.1820–1915	Romantic
c.1915–2000	20th Century
2000 +	21st Century

Too tired to practise?

Then do one of the following activities instead:

1. Practise away from the piano – just sit down with the piece you're learning and hear it through in your head. Think particularly about the character. Does it change?

2. Listen to some music – another piece by the same composer, a piece by another composer living at the same time, or some music in the same style.
   Your teacher will help.

3. Do a **PEP** analysis on the piece you are learning:
   P is for *problems* – decide what problems you still have to solve, technical or rhythmic for example. Make a note of them.
   E is for *expression* – what will you be trying to convey in your performance?
   P is for *practice* – the next practice! What in particular will you practise in your next session? Write your intentions down.

Notes